Broken Homes

Sandy Smith

Table of Contents

BROKEN HOMES

ACKNOWLEDGMENTS

It's never easy to be in a "BROKEN HOME". I know. I went through it when I was younger.

I want to say thank you to Fran Bolton when I was stuck on chapters and when I was so clueless on what else to add to this book. I came close on giving up on this book. Fran, thank you for being my backbone when I was so clueless on chapters.

There are people who were in a broken home like I have been. It wasn't easy for me to write this book. I have a wonderful family and friends who supported me when I was writing this book. This book is based on my past and things that I have remembered.

1 FOSTER HOME

There are children who have been placed in foster homes. Some of these children were placed because their parents had DVD's that young children shouldn't see (porn / nudity), or their parents couldn't take care of them (their parents may be drug users and/or their parents are mental), or for other reasons maybe. These children tended to be adopted.

Most of these children back then and even today were in broken homes. They tend to feel that they aren't cared for or loved, and much more. They have this empty place in their hearts because they don't have no one. That they are lost, lonely, and empty. Their emotions run low. There are people who don't understand them. The people who have been there know that feeling.

2 A GIRL ONLY 15 YEARS OLD

The girl was taken away from her mother. The girl didn't know what was happening to her until she realized that she was being placed in a foster home. Her parents had divorced at a young age. The young girl didn't see her dad and her sister. She felt like an outsider and out of place. All the girl wanted were parents who cared for her and loved her.

When she got to the place ... the girl, only 15 years old, didn't know how the family was going to treat her. After getting to know them, the girl really loved the family. She wished that this family would adopt her because that the girl, only 15 years old, fell in love with the family like the family did with her. The family still has a place in the girl's life, knowing that the girl had a bad childhood. All the girl wanted was to be loved.

She thought to herself, I have my whole life ahead of me. What would I like to be in ten to fifteen years? The girl, only 15, thought to herself that she'll take one day at a time. That it'll be there one day, what she wanted to be. The 15 year old thought about being an teacher, a singer, an artist, and a writer.

It wasn't easy to be a foster child, with me being in a foster home. I kept my head up high and I would be who I was. Learn what I needed to know. Most people thought that I would be a troubled person. I proved them wrong.

3 BEST BIRTHDAYS AND HOLIDAYS

A child turned a year older and had the best birthday ever. The sad thing is, the child didn't have her parents to celebrate her birthday with. That was okay with the child. The child celebrates her birthday with the people who cared for and loved her the most. The holidays without her parents were peaceful. The child didn't have to hear her parents fight. How one feels being without parents at a young age.

Children want their special day for their birthdays and holidays to be filled with happiness, love, joy, and much more. The children would "LOVE" to spend their birthdays and holidays with their parents, family, brothers, and the people that they care about.

4 HOW IT FEELS BEING WITHOUT PARENTS

There are children in this world who grew up without parents. The parents abandoned their children on the streets or wherever. These children never knew their parents. They had to learn things on their own.

There were people who brought these children in and taught them what they needed to know. Most of the children turned out well for themselves. They are either a doctor, a nurse, a lawyer, a cop, a fire fighter, a teacher, or whatever they became today.

5 LONELY

We tend to get lonely. Not a place to go where we want to be.

The only place we want to be is where people care about us. Those are the people who know how it is to be in a broken home. That person may have gone through it themselves and thought they would help bring other peoples' spirits up. Knowing that they may have lived that life.

There are days that we want to be by ourselves. To clear out our thoughts. We tend to want our space and need to sort out things.

6 HOME

When we think of home, we tend to think to ourselves that a home is a place where people care about us, people love us, and much more.

A home is where you are welcome at any time. A place where we feel safe at. Knowing that a person can unwind and to be themselves.

As you think to yourself. This is a place that I can call home. That you don't have to be abused. Home is a place that we supposed to feel safe, taken care of.

We don't want to be scared and we don't want to have to watch our backs.

7 MOTHER AND CHILDREN

When we young girls and older girls give birth to our children, we are so in love with our babies. As they grow up so fast, they don't need us as much. Sometimes when we have children, we're married to their dad and or just dating their dad. When we gals split up with him, he got custody of the children.

....As they grow older, all they know is their dad of the family. Their dad told them bunch of lies about you that aren't true. They don't want to hear the truth. They don't want to hear your side of the story.

One day when they get in their 30's or 40's they want to get the truth and they want to get to know you. Would it be too late, or would you close that chapter with your children? We as mothers have to make that choice for ourselves. It's not like we don't love our child or children. We had just missed so much in their lives the way it was.

I was laying in bed last night and these words came to me as I was thinking about my kids. How one feels being left without parents at a young age.

It's been hard on me and a lot of parents. I had never given up on my kids like they had on me. I know that I shouldn't care about my kids, but I do. Yes I had it hard.

8 PATIENCE

We all get so much going on in our lives. Most people try our patience. Knowing that we don't want to hear their life story. They need to know that we got our problems. You, other people, and I have been in broken homes. We all know we have our own problems.

There are days that we really don't have the patience to be around others. We tend to avoid people in any way we can. Knowing that we get so much going on and on our minds.

What I'm surprised though with myself. I stop and think about other people as well. I thought what I went through was rough. As I hear about other people from years past, theirs is worse.

It all depends who the person is.

9 OUR FIRST LOVE AND OUR FIRST KISS

When we don't go looking for a boy, then the boy finds the girl. When we (us girls) gets to know the boy, we take our time to make sure that he is the one. When we get to know him, we fall in love with that boy. That's when we realize that he became our first true love boyfriend. Once we feel comfortable with the boy, we might have our first kiss. It all depends where and when us girls would get our first kiss.

The tables can be turned, too. You never know what may happen and where it may be. Knowing that we have to choice wisely.

When us girls are at church, school, grocery store, festivals, or whatever it may be that's going on, we may look across the room, across the stage, and the boy may catch our eye. When we go to the boy, we get to talking and he mentions that he already has a girlfriend. He tells us that he has a brother who is looking for a girlfriend. That's when us girls found the one. We: us girl's) knew that he was the one. When we get to know him that we introduce him to our family. That your family knew that he was the one for you.

When you leave him alone to go to the next room, you never know what he is doing. Never know that your unmarried mother, your married sister, or your married cousin is talking to him while you are in the other room. You don't know what's going on until you come back into the room. That she is all over your boyfriend. You would'ved thought that he would push her away and he never did. He lead her on. That's when you go off on them.

When we (us girl's) are either pregnant or not pregnant that you go to your sister's and or cousin's house. As she is married while dating her husband's best friend and messing around with your boyfriend. As she asks you, your boyfriend, her and her boyfriend could go driving around because she has something to tell you. She tells you that she has been messing around with your boyfriend and all you want to do is beat her up. As she tells her boyfriend that she isn't in love with him because she's in love with her sister's or cousin's boyfriend. He is all mad.

Us girls who have sister's knows how it feels to be cheated on. We can't forgive our sisters and our cousins, knowing that we love them. We would NEVER see her as our sister and our cousin. They'll be dead to us inside. We'll never forgive what she had done to us and our mother. How could she do this to us girls?

Be careful who you trust with your boyfriend. Make sure you get a guy who would stand up to your mom, your sister, and your cousin.

Make sure that he really cares about you, loves you that much like he says he does, and respects you.

10 THE FIRST TIME YOU STARTED NOTICING BOYS

When we girls were younger, we weren't looking for a boyfriend. Granted, we were friends with boys. The boys tended to want to date them and you turn them down. We (us girls) weren't interested in dating. We didn't feel that we were ready to start dating boys. Most girls started dating at a young age. There's a lot of girls didn't start till they were 10 to 13 years of age. Plus there are girls who waited till they are 15 to 16 years of age. There are girls who are shy to be around boys.

11 THE BIRTH OF YOUR CHILDREN

We (us girls/gals) carry our babies for 9 months. When we have our babies that they bring us moms much love, charies, and much more.

The things that our babies do, we'll never forget. Wishing that we could have our cameras and camcorder with us. Knowing that we want to catch that moment.

12 SISTER'S LIES

As we were younger and living with our parent. Your older sister always tries to get you into trouble. As your parent checks up on you, they ask you if you had did it. You tell them no. When your sister tries to get you into trouble that she gets a spanking and or sent to a corner for her lies.

When we're older, as we are in different towns or states, your sister tells people that you pushed her down the steps or what ever it maybe. Knowing that you had "NEVER" seen her in 7 to 10 years.

You hear it from a relative that you had done this. They ask if it's true. You tell them it's a lie. That you don't drive and you are always broke. All your sister is doing is spreading lies about you. All she wants is you to sympathize for her.

13 TRUST

As we were younger that we got close to a person or people. Then we get used and hurt. We tend to believe our gut instinct. Never get close to a person or people. That's where we have trust issues from home, school, work, and or where ever it may be. Knowing that we came from a broken home.

We got to trust our gut instinct. Be careful who you let in. Get to know them before trusting him or her. Don't allow them to use you. Don't allow them to take advantage of you. Make sure to watch your back. Make wise decision on the things you do and much more.

SANDY SMITH

BROKEN HOMES

Made in the USA
Columbia, SC
17 July 2018